LIFE CYCLES

The
Kangaroo

Published by Raintree Steck-Vaughn Publishers, an imprint of Steck-Vaughn Company.

Acknowledgments
Project Editor: Helene Resky
Design Manager: Joyce Spicer
Consulting Editor: Kim Merlino
Consultant: Michael Chinery
Illustrated by David Webb
Map by David Webb
Designed by Ian Winton and Steve Prosser
Photography credits on page 32

Planned and produced by The Creative Publishing Company

Library of Congress Cataloging-in-Publication Data
    Crewe, Sabrina
    The kangaroo / Sabrina Crewe
      p.   cm. — (Life cycles)
    Includes index.
    Summary: Describes the life cycle, behavior, and habitat of the kangaroos.
    ISBN 0-8172-4370-4 (hardcover). — ISBN 0-8172-6233-4 (pbk.)
    1. Kangaroos—Juvenile literature.   2. Eastern grey kangaroo — Juvenile literature.
3. Kangaroos — Life cycles — Juvenile literature.   4. Eastern grey kangaroo — Life cycles — Juvenile literature. [1. Kangaroos. 2. Eastern grey kangaroo] I. Title.
II. Series: Crewe, Sabrina. Life cycles.
QL737.M35C74   1997
599.2 — dc20   96-4829
                        CIP   AC

1 2 3 4 5 6 7 8 9 0 LB 00 99 98 97 96
Printed and bound in the United States of America.

Words explained in the glossary appear in **bold** the first time they are used in the text.

LIFE CYCLES

The
Kangaroo

Sabrina Crewe

RSVP

RAINTREE
STECK-VAUGHN
PUBLISHERS
The Steck-Vaughn Company

Austin, Texas

The kangaroo is getting ready.

The kangaroo licks her **pouch** to make it clean. She is waiting for something to happen.

A baby kangaroo is born.

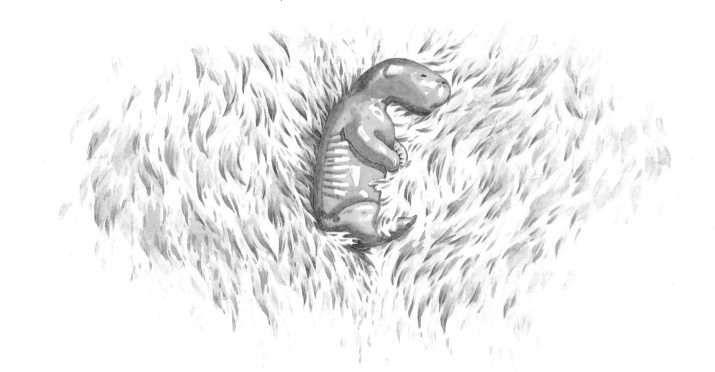

The baby is less than one inch
(2.5 cm) long. It looks like a little
jellybean. The baby cannot hear or
see yet, but it has strong front legs.

The baby kangaroo finds the pouch.

The baby has crawled up its mother's fur. It used its strong front legs to reach the pouch. Inside the pouch, it will find a **nipple**.

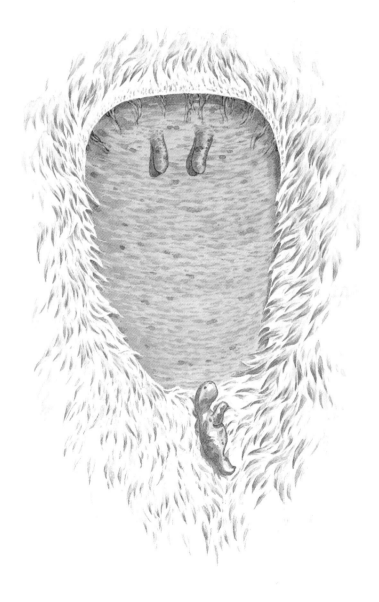

The baby kangaroo feeds on milk.

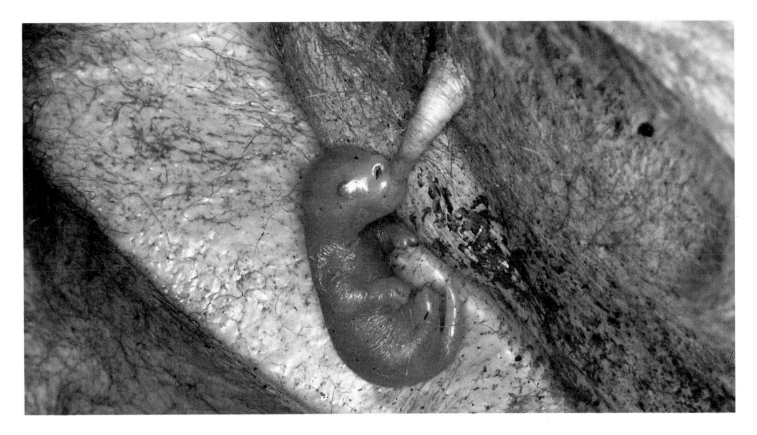

The baby is three weeks old. It
gets milk from its mother's nipple.
The baby kangaroo holds tightly
to the nipple for several months.

The baby kangaroo grows slowly.

The baby kangaroo is 12 weeks old.
It has grown a little bigger. You can
already see its claws. Soon the baby
will open its eyes.

The joey grows quickly.

The baby kangaroo is 18 weeks old.
It has grown much bigger and has
fur like its mother. Young kangaroos
are called **joeys**.

The joey looks out of the pouch.

The joey is nearly six months old. It pokes
its head out of the pouch. After a few more
weeks, it will come out for short periods.

The joey is out of the pouch.

The joey still drinks milk from its mother. There is a new baby in the pouch now, holding on to another nipple. When there is danger, the joey jumps back in, too!

The joey is grazing.

Now the joey is 18 months old. It **grazes** on grass and other plants. Kangaroos live in open grass and wooded places. They travel around in search of food.

The kangaroo is looking for food.

It can be very dry where kangaroos live.
Sometimes it is hard for the kangaroos
to find enough to eat. They search for
food in all kinds of places!

The joey and its mother live in a group.

Kangaroos live in small family groups.
Living in a group helps the kangaroos
guard against danger.

Most groups have a few females and joeys. There is often an adult male as well, especially in summer.

The dingo is hungry.

Dingoes are wild dogs that **prey** on kangaroos. The dingo has seen the kangaroos grazing. It is ready to attack.

The mother kangaroo senses danger.

The kangaroo stands up straight and stamps her back feet. She is warning her joey and the rest of the group. The kangaroos will have to escape quickly.

The kangaroos jump high!

The joey is almost two years old. It is
too big for its mother's pouch. It moves
fast by making big jumps to keep up
with its mother.

Some kangaroos can go 30 feet (9 m) in one jump. They can change direction with each jump to get away from enemies. They use their big tails for balance and to steer.

Male kangaroos are big.

When a male joey is fully grown, he is much bigger than his mother and other females. Kangaroos become adults when they are two years old.

The kangaroo has left his mother.

The kangaroo has made a group with
other young males. Young females stay
with their mothers' group or join another
family group.

The kangaroos are fighting.

The male kangaroos fight with their claws. They kick each other with their strong back legs. The kangaroos soon learn which of them is the strongest.

The male has a territory.

Each group of male kangaroos has its own area of land. The males often join up with female groups in their **territory**. But only the strongest males mate with the females.

The female is ready to mate.

The male kangaroo knows the female
is **fertile**. He is showing her he wants
to mate. A baby will be born five weeks
after they have mated.

Kangaroos need grazing land.

Farmers don't like kangaroos on their land. Hunters will kill kangaroos if they go where sheep are grazing. People can help kangaroos by leaving places where they can live safely and find food.

Parts of a Kangaroo

Kangaroos belong to a group of **mammals** called **marsupials**. Female marsupials have pouches in which they carry their young. Some marsupials eat other animals, but most eat plants.

Large tail
Used for balance, steering, and to rest on

Strong back legs and long feet
For jumping

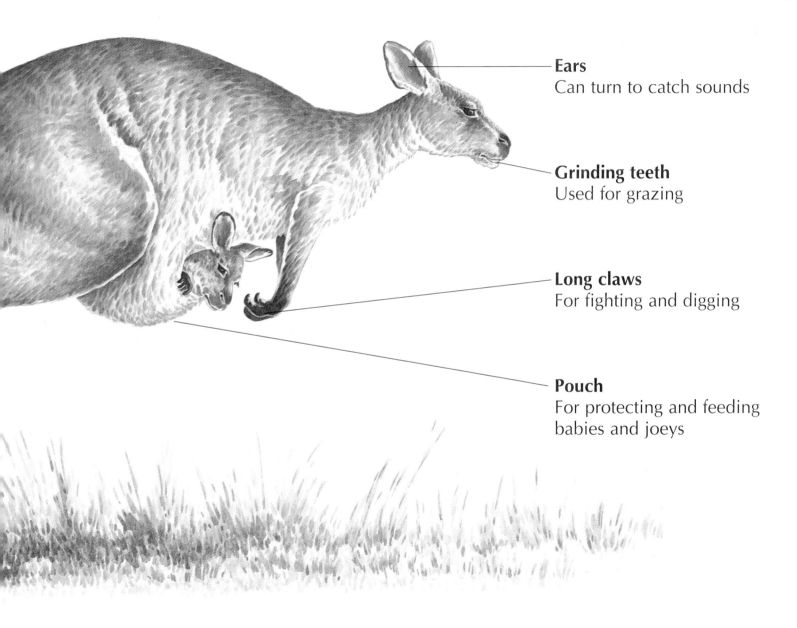

Ears
Can turn to catch sounds

Grinding teeth
Used for grazing

Long claws
For fighting and digging

Pouch
For protecting and feeding
babies and joeys

Other Marsupials

The kangaroo in this book is a gray kangaroo. Here are some other kangaroos and different kinds of marsupials.

Sugar glider

Koala

Wombat

Opossum

Rock wallaby

Tree kangaroo

Swamp wallaby

Red kangaroo

Where the Gray Kangaroo Lives

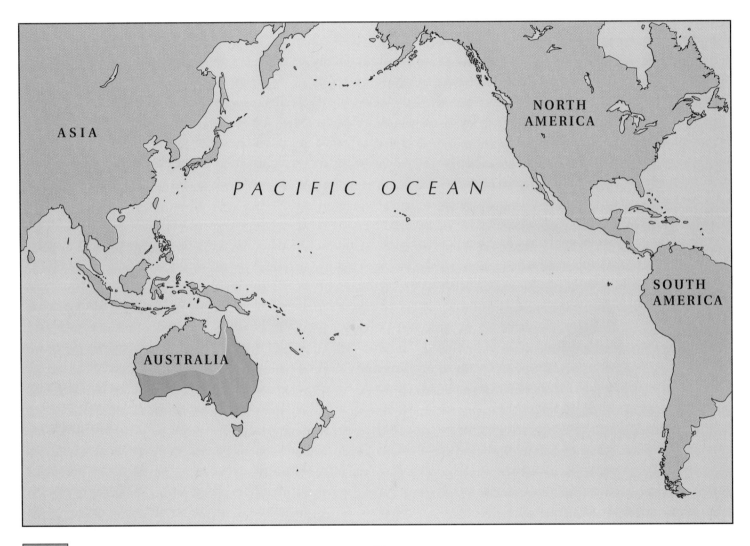

ASIA

NORTH AMERICA

PACIFIC OCEAN

SOUTH AMERICA

AUSTRALIA

Areas where the gray kangaroo lives

Glossary

Dingo A wild dog found in Australia

Fertile Ready to mate and produce young

Graze To feed on growing grass

Joey The young of a kangaroo

Mammal A kind of animal that usually has fur and feeds its young with milk

Marsupial A type of mammal that has a pouch

Nipple The part of a mammal's body with which a female gives milk to her young

Pouch The pocket-shaped part of a female marsupial's body used for carrying and feeding its young

Prey To hunt or kill another animal for food

Territory An area of land that an animal defends as its own

Index

Baby **5, 6, 7, 8, 11, 24**
Claws **8, 22, 27**
Dingo **16**
Family **14–15, 21, 23, 24**
Fighting **22**
Food **7, 11, 12, 13, 26**
Grazing **12, 25**
Hunters **25**
Joey **9, 10, 11, 12, 15, 17, 18**
Jumping **18–19**
Legs **5, 6, 22, 26**
Mammal **26**
Marsupial **26, 28–29**
Mating **23, 24**
Nipple **6, 7**
Pouch **4, 6, 10, 11, 26, 27**
Sheep **25**
Tail **19, 26**
Territory **23**

Photography credits